DJUSD
Public Schools
Library Protection Act 1998

D1735994

WORLD OF SPORTS
TAE KWON DO

Published by Smart Apple Media
123 South Broad Street, Mankato, Minnesota 56001

Copyright © 2001 Smart Apple Media.
International copyrights reserved in all countries.
No part of this book may be reproduced in any form without
written permission from the publisher.

Photography: cover—ALLSPORT/Joe Patronite;
pages 4–5, 15—CORBIS/Roger Ressmeyer;
page 7—CORBIS/Macduff Everton;
page 8—CORBIS/Asian Art & Archaeology, Inc.;
page 9—CORBIS/Lowell Georgia;
page 11, 17—ALLSPORT/Gerard Plancheniault;
page 14—CORBIS/Dean Conger;
page 18–19, 28–29, 31—CORBIS/Michael S. Yamashita;
page 20—CORBIS/Ted Spiegel;
page 22, 25—INDEX STOCK/Todd Powell;
page 23—ALLSPORT/David Leah;
page 24—CORBIS/Phil Schermeister;
page 27—ALLSPORT/Mike Powell

Design and Production by EvansDay Design

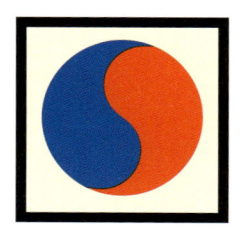

LIBRARY OF CONGRESS CATALOGING-IN-PUBLICATION DATA

Olson, Marcy.
Tae kwon do / by Marcy Olson.
p. cm. — (World of sports)
Includes index.
Summary: Presents the history, principles, gym etiquette,
belts, and vocabulary of the ancient art and sport of
tae kwon do.
ISBN 1-887068-55-4
1. Tae kwon do—Juvenile literature. [1. Tae kwon do.] I. Title.
II. Series: World of sports (Mankato, Minn.)
GV1114.9.O57   2000
796.815'3—dc21   98-33676

First edition

9 8 7 6 5 4 3 2 1

TAE KWON DO

MARCY OLSON

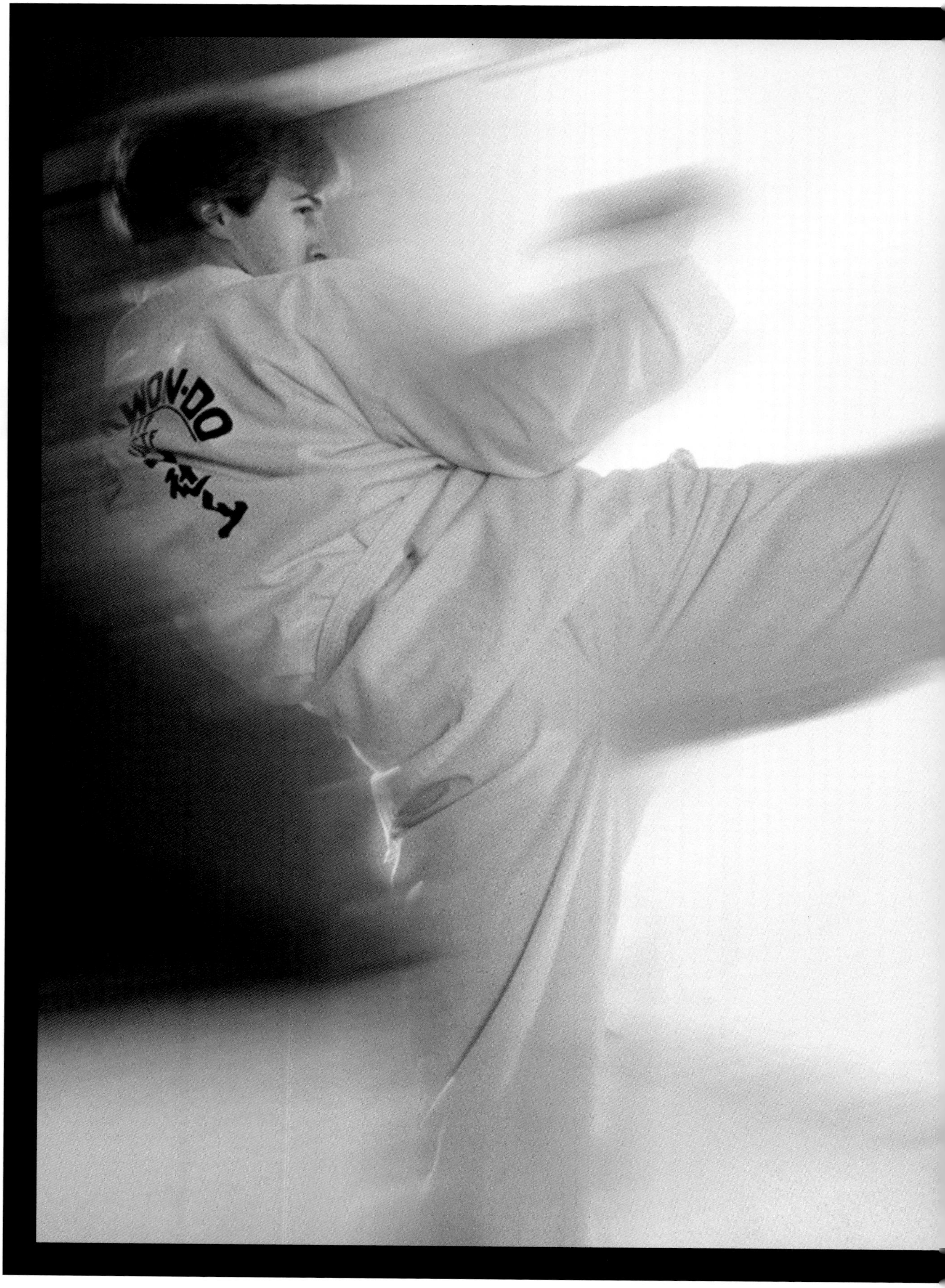
WON·DO

> *Taekwondo exercises the entire body, including the vital organs, giving the student a high level of motivation both in the gym and in life.... Taekwondo creates spiritual balance through physical activity. It originated from the efforts to balance mind and body through harmony of power, actions, and the need to control the mind.*
>
> Jeong Rok Kim

The Art of Kicking and Punching

IN TAE KWON DO, THE wonder of an ancient **martial art** comes to life. From the snap of breaking boards to the shatter of bricks, from pulse-quickening yells to blood-curdling shrieks, and from twirling chrome knives to spinning acrobatic kicks, tae kwon do is not a typical sport. It involves the technical acrobatics and precision of gymnastics, the speed and power of boxing, and the physical demands and agility of basketball. Few other sports involve stacks of wooden boards broken with a human hand or foot, or columns of cement blocks crushed by a man's forehead.

Tae kwon do is a martial art from Korea whose name means "the art of kicking and punching." *Tae* means "to strike with the feet," *Kwan* means "destroying with the hand or fist," and *Do* means "way" or "method." Tae kwon do is believed to be one of the oldest oriental arts of unarmed self-defense.

No ranking system existed in the martial arts until 1883, when Jigoro Kano, the founder of judo, awarded senior rankings to two of his best students. Skilled judo students did not begin wearing black belts until 1886.

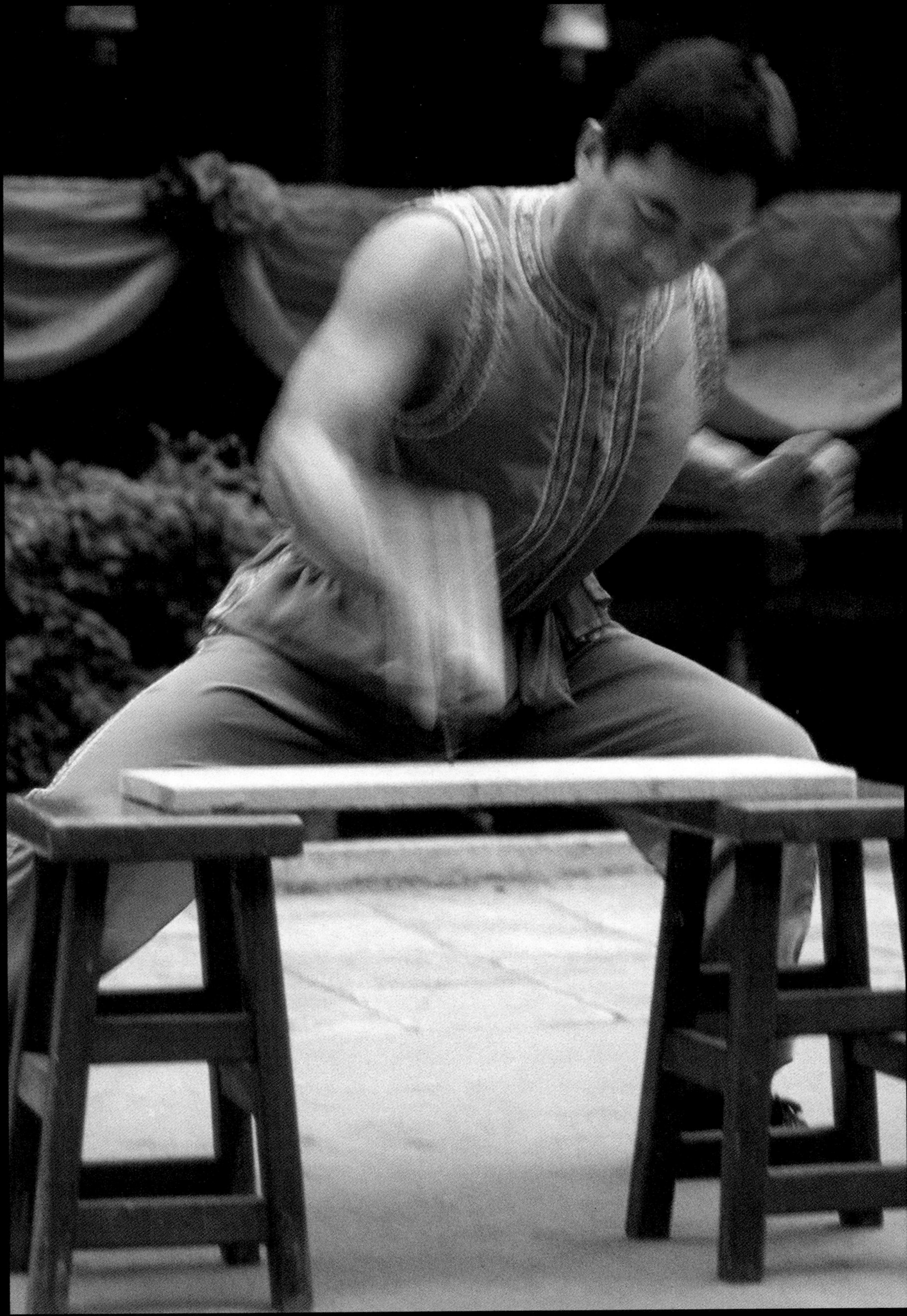

The roots of tae kwon do date back to around 2330 B.C.—more than 4,000 years ago. The Korean people often had to fight to protect or regain their political independence. This struggle created a fierce warrior spirit, intense national loyalty, and an indomitable spirit. About 2,000 years ago, the **Hwa Rang Do** was formed. It established a code of honor that included the five principles of tae kwon do: loyalty to one's nation, respect for one's parents, courage in battle, using violence with discretion, and never needlessly taking the life of a person or animal.

In its early forms, tae kwon do was an ancient art of defense passed down within families from one generation to the next. Schools became highly selective, allowing

Since its origin thousands of years ago, tae kwon do has been a means of gaining peace and wisdom as well as self-defense techniques.

martial art any of various ancient arts of combat or self-defense that originated in eastern Asia

Hwa Rang Do a Korean military and educational organization that established the principles behind modern tae kwon do

kwan the Korean word for a tae kwon do school or organization branch

master a head teacher in a tae kwon do gym; a martial artist who has a first degree black belt or higher

only the best students to train and eventually serve as apprentices in instructing the next generation of students.

At the turn of the 20th century, Korea was occupied by the Japanese, who outlawed tae kwon do. The art then went underground, where people practiced in secret to keep it alive. In 1945, when Korea was liberated, a number of tae kwon do **kwans** were formed and took steps to revitalize this ancient and traditional martial art. Soon after, the art was given its current name and organized under 10 schools founded by tae kwon do **masters**.

Tae kwon do has since flourished and spread in popularity, becoming the national sport of Korea. It is included in school curriculums from first grade through college and is required for military service. Tae kwon do, as most American students of the art know it, was first brought to the United States in the late 1950s.

Near the end of the seventh century A.D., the Hwa Rang Do—the group of men that established the central principles of tae kwon do—changed from a military organization to a school that specialized in poetry and music.

The Tae kwon do Association, an organization whose goal was to bring different schools together, was recognized by the Korean government in 1965. The association is headquartered in a beautiful building called the Kukkiwon, which was built in Seoul, Korea, in 1972. The Kukkiwon houses the central governing body of traditional tae kwon do schools. It also serves as a research center for the advancement of tae kwon do as a scientific sport, provides a testing center for black belt promotions, and is used to hold national and international championships. Dr. Un Yong Kim, the highest-ranking tae kwon do black belt in the world, was elected president of the Kukkiwon.

In May 1973, the first World Tae kwon do Championships were held in Seoul. Of the 30 participating countries, Korea took first place in the team competition, the United States took second, and Mexico and the Republic of China tied for third. Following this tournament, all of the officials representing their countries at the event formed the World Tae kwon do Federation (WTF) and elected Dr. Un Yong Kim as the president. Signing all official, internationally-recognized black belt certifications and presiding over all WTF schools are two responsibilities of the WTF president.

A TAE KWON DO MASTER DEMONSTRATES A HIGH KICK TO TWO STUDENTS. SUCH ADVANCED MOVES REQUIRE YEARS OF PRACTICE.

Kwan Jang Nim *a Korean term for master instructors who head schools or branches of the World Tae kwon do Federation*

The International Black Belt Federation (IBBF) is the organization of **Kwan Jang Nim**, black belts, and students who practice the tae kwon do style of Grand Master Moo Young Yun. The IBBF—one of the largest tae kwon do organizations in the U.S.—has schools in North Dakota, South Dakota, Minnesota, Alaska, Florida, and Washington.

Only in the last few decades have women been permitted to practice tae kwon do. Today, women and girls make up almost a third of the tae kwon do population worldwide. A special organization for female tae kwon do students and masters has been established in Seoul. This organization publishes a quarterly newsletter addressing the concerns of female martial artists around the world. The women's tae kwon do president is Choon Hee Seo, a ninth degree black belt.

Each belt color in tae kwon do signifies a student's skill level and represents a new stage in his or her development. White represents innocence; yellow, a plant growing roots; green, a plant growing leaves; blue, a plant growing toward the sky; red, a warning of danger; and black, maturity, or the opposite of white.

A Noble Sport

The development of tae kwon do skills is as much spiritual as it is physical. Tae kwon do teaches students to exercise sacrifice, self-restraint, humility, patience, and forgiveness. The physical skills taught to tae kwon do students are not to be used to cause pain, but to actively prevent it. A student learns to resist hurting others, even though he possesses the skills to cause great harm. As tae kwon do masters emphasize, the ultimate good lies not in winning a hundred battles, but in overcoming a man or an entire army without conflict.

*Between 1400 and 1900 A.D., tae kwon do virtually disappeared from Korea's military training. The teachings of **Confucius**, which became the dominant religion at the time, stated that the higher class should devote itself to poetry and music. Only the lower class was expected to practice martial arts.*

Tae kwon do has been described by many experts as a state of mind. The art goes beyond physical speed, strength, and grace. It is a way of life that aims to do anything perfectly, peacefully, and humbly. There are three basic goals in tae kwon do: to achieve a concentration of power, to learn more about one's self, and to use that knowledge in everyday life.

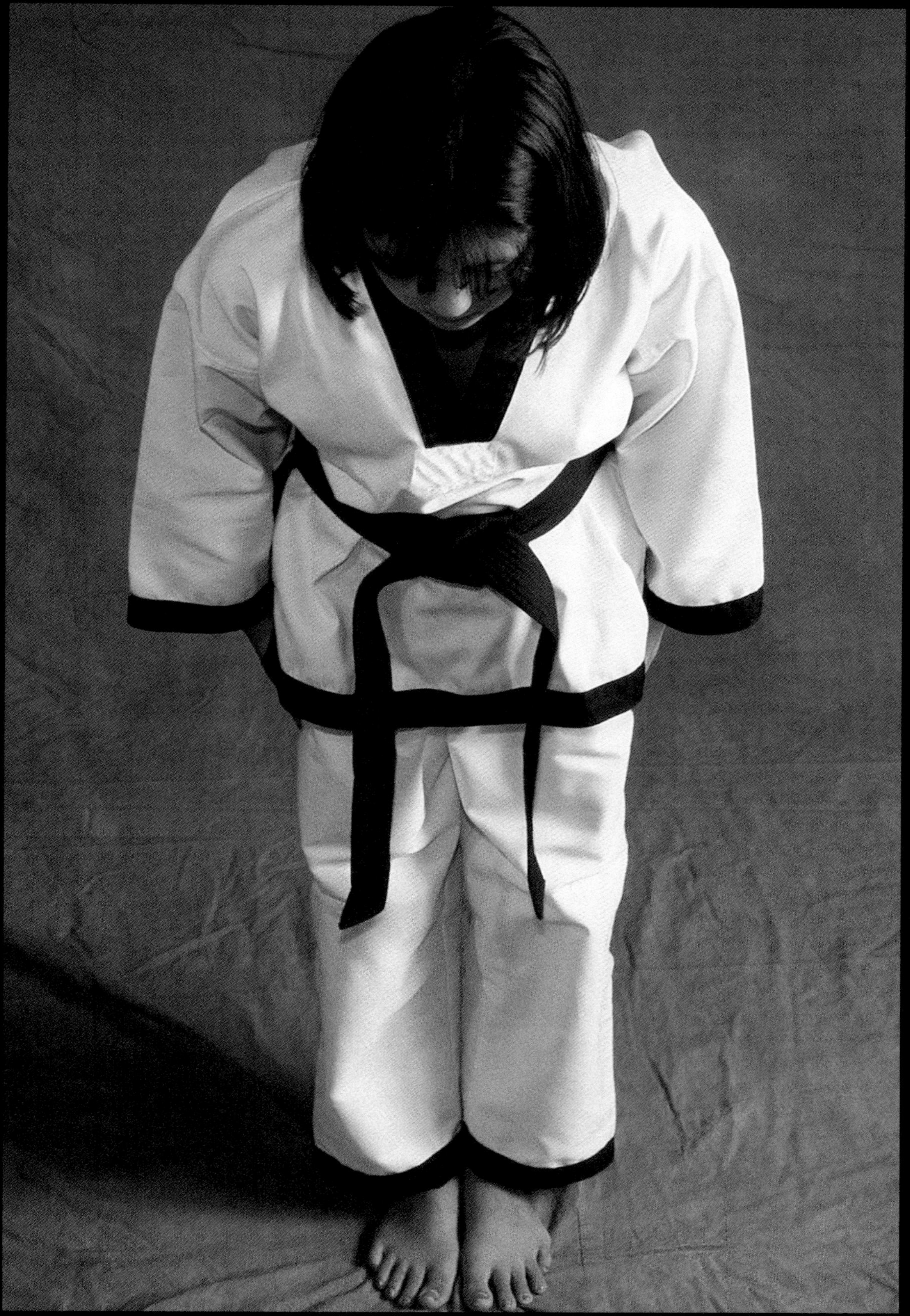

One of tae kwon do's most important principles is its reverence for all forms of life. Although tae kwon do can give a person power, it is a power that carries serious responsibility. Tae kwon do students learn to use the minimum force necessary to subdue an assailant. Like all martial arts, tae kwon do is meant to be used only for self-defense—never for aggressive attack.

The modern sport of tae kwon do serves as a means of exercise for both the body and the mind. Properly practiced and studied, it purifies the spirit as it trains a person's muscles and focus. It enables a person to concentrate on the movement of the body and to regulate his breathing, making him more aware of his physical capabilities.

Students of tae kwon do learn to have courtesy, integrity, self-control, perseverance, and a never-say-die attitude. These **tenets** are the foundation on which tae kwon do was built. Every aspect of the martial art aims to help individuals become strong—both physically and mentally—and moral people.

ALTHOUGH TAE KWON DO IS A SUPERB FORM OF PHYSICAL EXERCISE, IT ALSO INVOLVES MEDITATION AND THE QUEST FOR GREATER INNER PEACE.

Confucius *a Chinese philosopher whose religious teachings stress peace*

tenet *a principle that is believed to be true*

Many law enforcement officers and employees of such government branches as the Central Intelligence Agency (CIA) are taught tae kwon do.

Tae kwon do students should establish long-range goals for themselves, demonstrate maturity and good sportsmanship, and represent the martial arts well. A good martial artist strives for constant improvement, recognizing that there are always skills to be learned. Students should also follow the rules of etiquette and be a good example for others to follow at home, school, and all social functions.

Physical evidence of early forms of tae kwon do in Korea dates back to the first century B.C. The walls of tombs from that time period have been found decorated with paintings of men in fighting stances.

Tae kwon do Training

BEGINNING STUDENTS LEARN the basic tae kwon do techniques, as well as patience, humility, and respect for the art. Students are ranked with one of 10 belt colors. White, representing innocence and purity, is the belt color of beginners. The belt colors change as a student's abilities increase. Students are taught to focus on the development of their own skills, rather than measuring their progress against that of other students.

Tae kwon do training includes a type of floor exercise known as **Poomsae**, which means "patterns" or "forms." In this training, a student performs a number of consecutive moves in a certain order against an imaginary opponent. Each movement in the exercise is part of a detailed set of standards developed through centuries of tradition in Korea and is intended to improve the student's flexibility, balance, and control. Tae kwon do students are also expected to learn the art's terminology,

The Korean Tigers are a national demonstration team that trains at the Kukkiwon and puts on astounding shows for audiences. They perform incredibly difficult breaks using acrobatics, pyramids, mounts, flips, and props such as chairs, flames, and springboards.

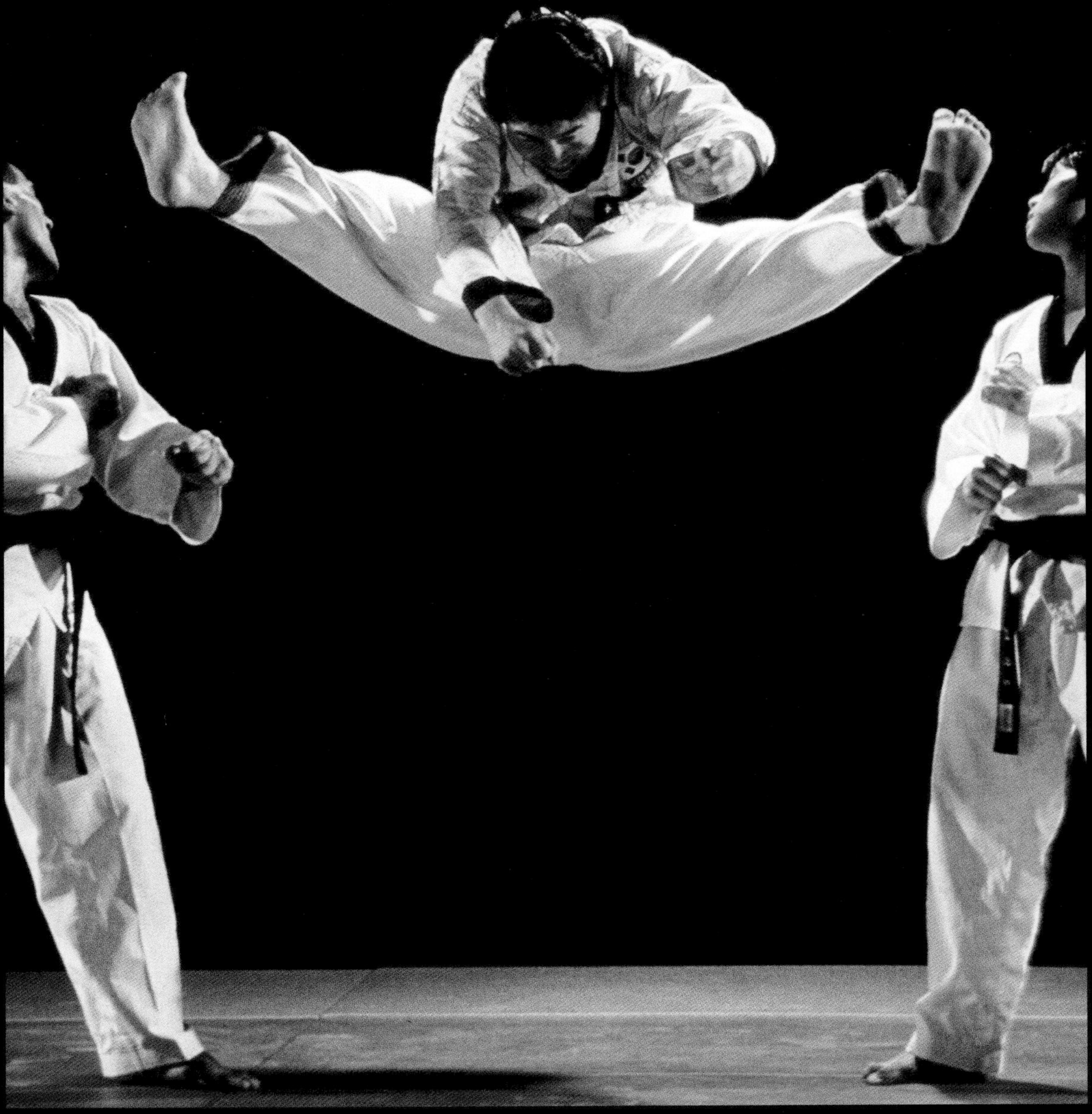

which includes many techniques with Korean names. A number of tenets must also be memorized and recited by students at test times as part of the art's mental training.

During physical training, students work on kicks and punches that are put to the test at promotion time. To acquire more-advanced belts, students are asked to break a board or two with a single kick or punch. Throughout the training, students practice their strikes using only punching bags. **Breaking** represents an obstacle that students must "mentally" overcome.

Young tae kwon do students, fully covered by protective gear, spar in a tournament in Seoul, Korea.

Although tae kwon do students spend much of their time striking pads, sparring competitions are a critical part of training as well.

Poomsae a form of tae kwon do practice in which a person executes various techniques against an imaginary opponent

breaking the act of breaking boards, bricks, and similar objects to prove mastery of techniques

vital points places on the body that have a high number of nerves just beneath the skin; even slight impacts to these areas can cause pain

Adam's apple the projection in the front of the neck formed by the top part of the windpipe

solar plexus the pit of the stomach

Tae kwon do students are taught which areas of an opponent's body are most sensitive to attack during combat. A trained master knows hundreds of these **vital points**, but some of the most vulnerable parts are the temples, the neck artery, the **Adam's apple**, and the **solar plexus**. Strong and accurate strikes to these parts can be crippling or even fatal.

As students advance, they may also learn fighting techniques using various weapons, which are introduced to broaden a student's ability and experience. Weapons may include the **nunchuku**, the **bo**, and the sword. Self-defense techniques for specific situations, including escapes from choke holds

Most tae kwon do competition matches consist of three rounds of three minutes, with one-minute rests between rounds. In matches between elementary or middle school contestants, however, bouts are shortened to three rounds of two minutes.

19

and knife attacks, are also taught to advanced students.

Tae kwon do students need to meet certain expectations. They must strive for a complete understanding of all aspects of the art. They are encouraged to practice as often as possible—this is the secret to lifelong learning. Students are also expected to dedicate themselves to the promotion of tae kwon do, which may mean participating in tournaments and demonstrations, helping out at **open gym**, or teaching less-skilled students.

At a surface level, tae kwon do appears to be a violent

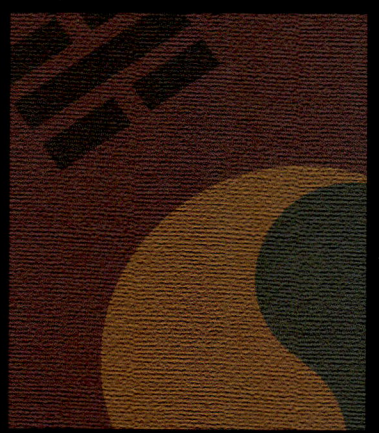

In the late 1950s, Korean soldiers became the first students of modern tae kwon do when the art became a mandatory part of army training in Korea. Policemen and air force troops also had to learn tae kwon do.

nunchuku *two short sticks connected by a chain or rope that are used as a weapon*

bo *a straight stick about one inch (2.5 cm) in diameter and more than four feet (1.2 m) in length that is used as a weapon*

sport. Its techniques, when used by a trained master, can seriously injure or even kill an opponent. Punches, kicks, elbow blows, and smashes with the head can break boards, bricks, cement blocks—and bones.

Yet tae kwon do is a peaceful art that emphasizes harmony with nature, one another, and the universe. With this philosophy, the more techniques students learn, the more they desire to use them wisely. The art of tae kwon do is meant to develop a student's sense of mercy, kindness, modesty, and calmness. As they master physical skills, students also build character and gain confidence—traits that all accomplished tae kwon do warriors possess.

BREAKING BOARDS OR BRICKS, A MEANS OF TESTING ONE'S SKILL LEVEL, IS ONE OF THE MOST VISUALLY IMPRESSIVE FEATS IN TAE KWON DO.

INCREASED BALANCE, FLEXIBILITY, AND QUICKNESS ARE JUST A FEW OF THE PHYSICAL BENEFITS GAINED THROUGH TAE KWON DO PRACTICE.

open gym *a scheduled time during which tae kwon do students can voluntarily come to a gym and work on techniques in an informal setting*

Climbing the Ranks

To advance to a higher tae kwon do belt, students must demonstrate mastery of the techniques, forms, and skills taught in the gym during practices. They must be able to recite mottos, terminology, and information about the history of tae kwon do. Students are also expected to learn about the Korean and American flags and what each design element represents. At the end of the test, students must successfully perform a break of boards, bricks, or similar items using a technique they have learned during the most recent training period. This break serves as proof that the student has mastered the material and is ready for the next level.

Illegal strikes or acts in tae kwon do competition are divided into two categories: Kyonggo (warning penalty) and the more serious Gam-jeom (deduction penalty). Kyonggo penalties include such offenses as grabbing or pushing an opponent, while Gam-jeom penalties include such acts as attacking a fallen opponent or displaying poor sportsmanship.

A new belt and certificate are awarded to the student upon successful completion of the test material. Most students test for new belts in intervals of about three months. Students, who begin as "no-belts," first

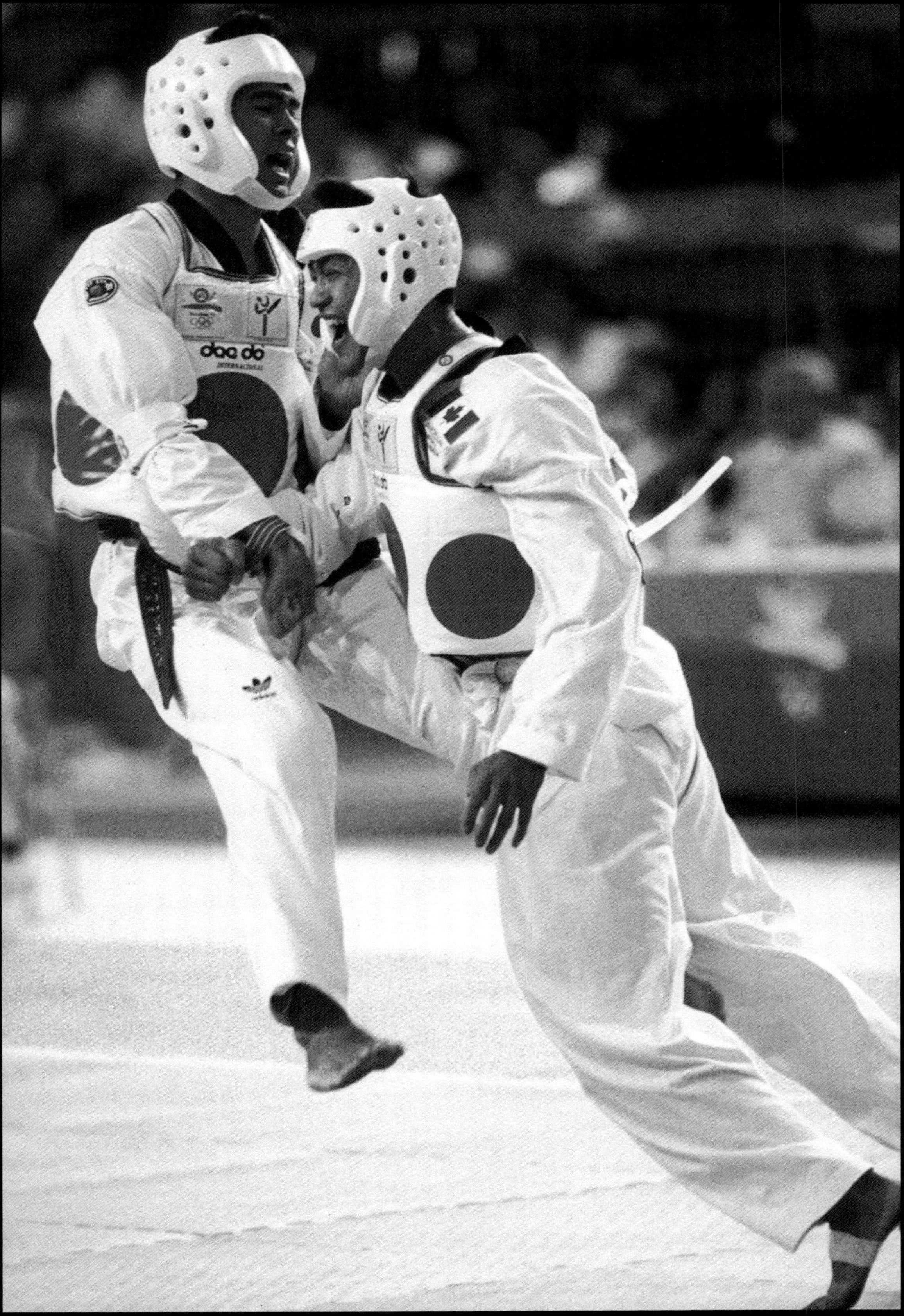
dae do

earn a white belt and gradually advance through the ranks in this order: orange, yellow, green, blue, purple, purple-stripe, brown, red, and finally black. A younger tae kwon do student who moves quickly up the ranks may achieve a **Poom**, while an accomplished older child or adult may be promoted to a **Dan**. As students advance and training techniques become more difficult, the time between tests may be longer. Students who earn a red belt may train for more than a year before they are ready to test for their black belt.

After reaching black belt status, a student may take years to advance through the black belt ranks. Many master instructors have achieved fourth or fifth degree rankings in their tae kwon do training. Very few black belts are awarded

Poom *the Korean word for a junior (16 years old or younger) black belt*

Dan *the Korean word for an adult black belt*

TAE KWON DO STUDENTS ARE ENCOURAGED TO INCREASE THEIR KNOWLEDGE OF THE ART BY OBSERVING OTHERS, INCLUDING MORE ADVANCED STUDENTS.

No matter what a person's age or size, tae kwon do is an excellent way to stay fit and gain confidence.

the advanced rankings of seventh and eighth degrees. The ninth and tenth degrees are even more rare and are considered the highest honors for lifetime achievements in tae kwon do. Dr. Un Yong Kim, president of the World Tae kwon do Federation, has an 11th degree ranking—the highest in the world.

Tae kwon do students must learn Korean terms and numbers as part of their training. The numbers one through ten in the Korean language are Hana, Dul, Set, Net, Da Sut, Ya Sut, Il Gup, Ya Dul, I Hop, Yul.

Tae kwon do tests also involve oral exams, which include the recitation of Korean terminology and numbers. Since many of the instructions in a traditional tae kwon do gym are given in Korean, it is important for students to learn the terminology early. An understanding of Korean terminology is critical when dignitaries and high-ranking instructors from Korea visit a gym.

Fighting for Fun

STUDENTS STRIVE TO improve their techniques in **sparring** matches and **form competition**. To spar, competitors wear protective gear that includes pads for the hands, shins, elbows, and feet, head gear, chest protectors, and mouth guards. Rules prohibit such tactics as tackling, grabbing, or striking with the knee.

Students of tae kwon do must understand the design elements of the American flag, called "Old Glory." Its 13 horizontal stripes represent the 13 original colonies. The color red represents the blood shed in war to preserve freedom, and the color white represents the purity of the United States' ideals.

The sparring match is scored by as many as five judges. Points are awarded for accurate kicks or powerful punches to "legal" areas of an opponent's body. Legal strikes include punches to the **trunk** and kicks to the face, with two points awarded for accurate kicks to the side of the head. Illegal strikes include punches to the face, kicks to the body, and attacks to the back. Points may also be taken away for illegal strikes below the lower abdomen, malicious attacks, or unsportsmanlike conduct. Some organizations also allow full-contact competition in which

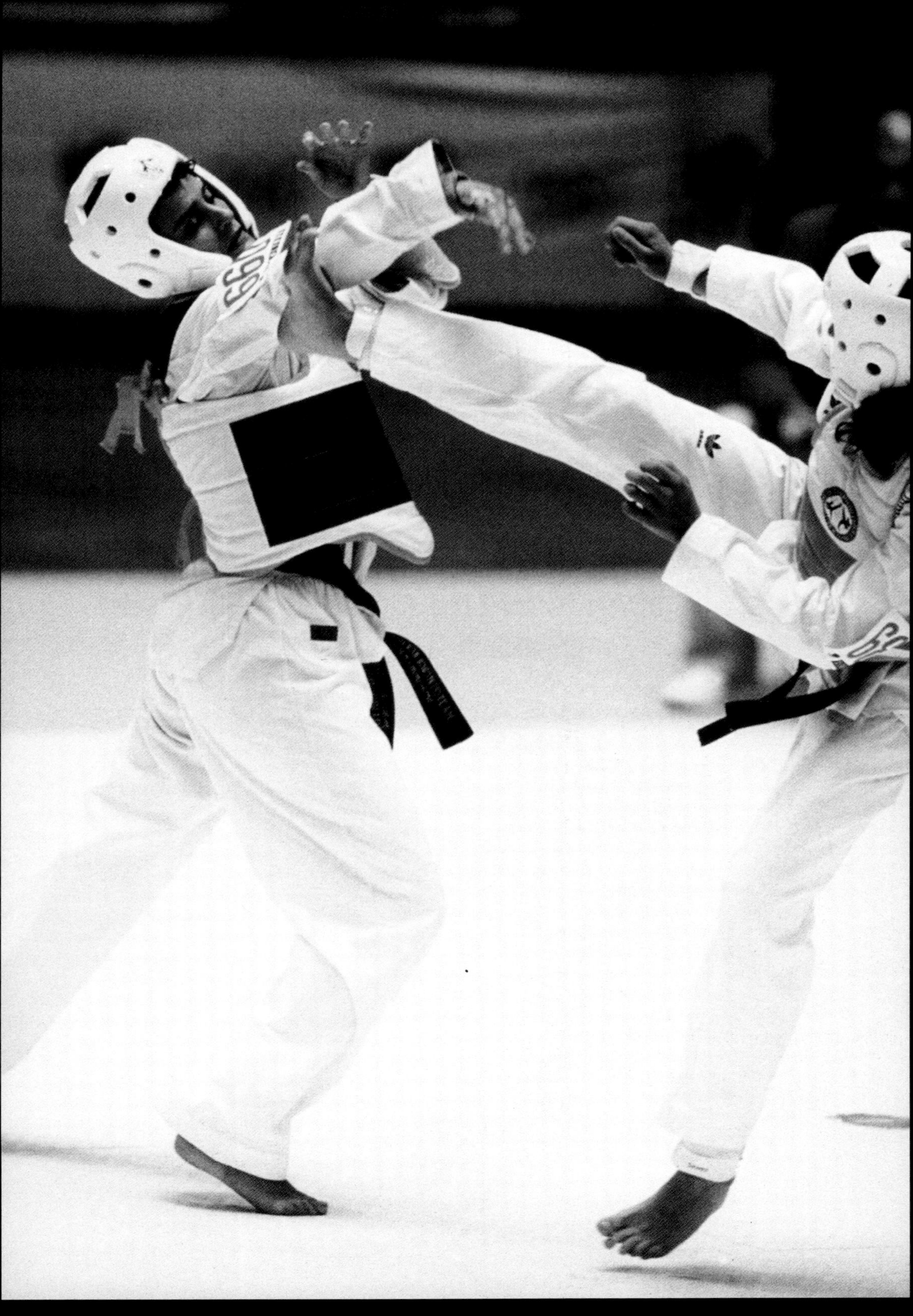

participants fight for three three-minute rounds and try to win by scoring points or knocking out their opponent.

Form competition puts students of the same age and rank together. Competitors demonstrate their form, or "pattern," for a panel of judges who rank first degree black belt or higher. The judges award a pattern 5 to 10 points using increments of one-half point. All scores are totaled, and the highest total wins. Judges determine their scores on the height of kicks, accuracy of strikes, and confidence shown.

Breaking is another competition in tae kwon do tournaments. Students of similar ages, abilities, and ranks are given the same "break" option. Beginners may have to use a

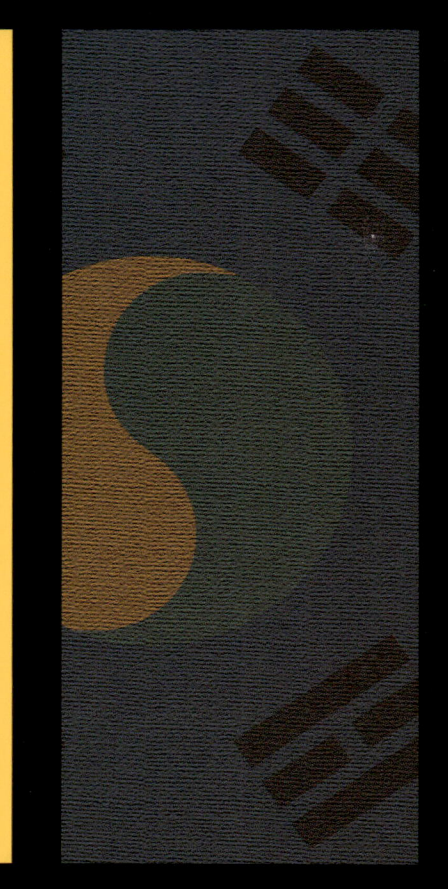

sparring *a controlled fight designed to showcase competitors' skills and techniques*

form competition *the demonstration of various techniques in front of a panel of judges in a tournament setting*

trunk *the abdomen and chest regions on a person's body*

TOURNAMENTS ARE INTENSE AND COMPETITIVE, BUT THEY ARE ALSO MEANT TO BE FUN EVENTS AND AN OPPORTUNITY TO SHOWCASE ONE'S SKILLS.

single kick to break one board, while advanced students may have to break five boards using three different strikes.

Although students are not required to attend every tournament, attendance and participation is an important part of tae kwon do training. By observing others and participating in healthy competition, students can better themselves in ways that are not possible by training alone in the gym. Tae kwon do students can also bring home some trophies and medals, as well as a greater sense of pride.

Part of tae kwon do training involves learning the design elements of the Korean flag, the "Tae Guk." Its white background represents purity, while the circle in the center stands for conflicting opposites such as good and evil. Four symbols are positioned in the corners of the flag that represent heaven, water, earth, and fire.

To make tournaments as fair as possible, competitors are always grouped in small sections by comparable rank and physical size. Weight classes at more advanced levels of competition range from finweight—110 pounds (50 kg) for males and 95 pounds (43 kg) for females—to heavyweight—more than 183 pounds (83 kg) for males and 154 pounds (70 kg) for females. Tournament directors at all levels do their best to give each participant the most evenly-matched competition possible.

Competition is beneficial at all ranks. Tournaments may be held all over a region, with a number of "family tournaments" held closer to home. These family tournaments involve all schools in a program and are held to familiarize students with the tournament experience. This competition increases their confidence and generates excitement for larger-scale tae kwon do competition.

The benefits of healthy tae kwon do competition are numerous. Tournaments provide a safe environment in which to seek new challenges and sharpen skills. The experience encourages students to observe the techniques and strategies of their opponents, gaining knowledge about the art. Tae kwon do competition also stresses the importance of good sportsmanship and helps build friendships by bringing together students from a wide area. Form competitions require competitors to present themselves verbally and physically in front of judges, their seniors, black belts, family, and spectators—an experience that builds confidence.

Tournaments are always conducted in a safe manner. Although tae kwon do is a serious and disciplined contact sport, every effort is made to ensure that the competition is light and fun.

Tae kwon do's vital points, or targeted strike areas on the body, are categorized by the vulnerability of each area. Strikes to the shin or elbow inflict moderate pain, the weakest attack, while blows to the head or certain arteries are classified as fatal, the deadliest attacks.

In 1984, tae kwon do competition was taken to the ultimate level when the International Olympic Committee (IOC) made the World Tae kwon do Federation a member of the Olympic Games. Tae kwon do was introduced to the world as a demonstration sport for the first time at the 1988 Olympic Games in Seoul, Korea. In 1986, the art was included as an official sport in the Asian Games, South American Games, and

TAE KWON DO TOURNAMENTS ARE CEREMONIAL EVENTS IN WHICH STUDENTS HELP CELEBRATE THE HISTORY AND TRADITION OF THE SPORT.

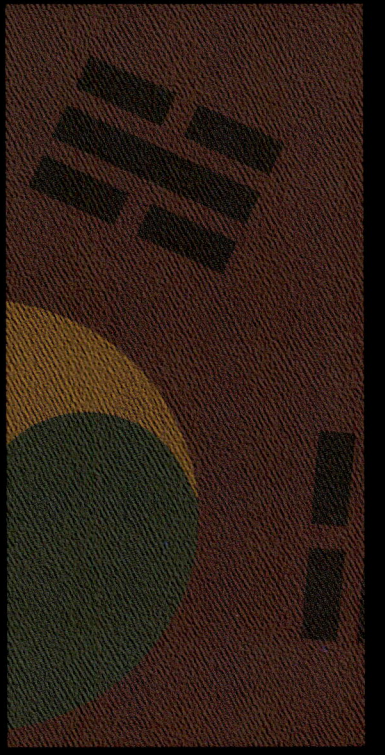

Bolivian Games. Tae kwon do was accepted to be an official Olympic sport for the first time at the 2000 Games in Sydney, Australia. The World Tae kwon do Federation is the only organization with IOC permission to supervise all international tae kwon do activities.

Each year, international interest in tae kwon do grows as both a spectator sport and a physical activity. By the end of the 20th century, there were more than 100 million students in 115 countries practicing tae kwon do. At 4,000 years old, the art of tae kwon do seems to get better as it gets older.

INDEX

A
American flag 22, 26

C
Choon Hee Seo 11
Confucius 12, 14

G
Gam-jeom 22

H
Hwa Rang Do 8, 9

I
International Black Belt Federation (IBBF) 10–11
International Olympic Committee (IOC) 30–31

J
Jeong Rok Kim 5
Jigoru Kano 6
judo 6

K
Korea 6, 8
Korean flag 22, 29
Korean terminology 18, 22, 25
Korean Tigers 16
Kukkiwon 9–10, 16
kwan SEE tae kwon do schools
Kwan Jang Nim 11
Kyonggo 22

M
Moo Young Yun 11

O
Olympic Games 30–31

P
Poomsae 16

T
tae kwon do
  belts 10, 11, 16, 22, 24–25
  history 6–8, 12, 15
  masters 9, 19, 21, 24–25
  protective equipment 26
  schools 8, 9–11
  tenets 12, 14–15, 20
  tournaments 19, 22, 26, 28–30, 31
  training 16, 18–21, 22, 24–25, 26
  weapons 6, 19–20
Tae kwon do Association 9–10

U
Un Yong Kim 10, 25

V
vital points 19, 30

W
World Tae kwon do Championships 10
World Tae kwon do Federation (WTF) 10, 25, 30, 31